this book is dedicated
to you...
love from me.
xoxo

YOU Need TO EXIST

A BOOK TO LOVE AND DESTROY!

BY YUNGBLUD

HAPPY
BOOKS
PLACE

Hello...

I never thought I was any good at reading books, but here I am fucking writing one.

Books always signified silence to me. A big cold room with some librarian telling me to be quiet, or a fireplace burning in the countryside waiting for the post man to come. Contemplating blowing my brains out just for something to do. The truth is I hate silence, I'm terrified of it. I've been running from it my whole life. My mind is too loud, you see. I've got too many thoughts, my brain can't keep up.
I feel like I've been playing catch up with myself ever since the first time 11 thoughts popped into my head at once.

All I ever wanted to do was exist. Like, REALLY exist. I know that I literally exist. I can feel my skin and the ground beneath my feet and shit. What I mean is that I wanted to exist in a way that meant someone would remember me when I met them in the street, or that something I said would imprint on their mind for a while. Growing up I just never felt like I did. I felt alone, invisible, overlooked, as if my point of view was "almost brilliant" but just the slightest bit disingenuous. That I should be "seen and not heard" - a teacher literally said that to me once. Surprise, surprise, he was old, white and taught P.E.

I have made it my life's mission to find people who felt like me - silenced by the ignorant, colourful but forced to live in black and white. I started that with Yungblud and it's grown into something way bigger than I could have ever imagined. A creative and unique community that celebrates what makes each person different. It's become a movement that empowers people to explore their identities, to truly be themselves. I want this book to go beyond music, to be another adventure and bring as many of you together as possible.

This book will give you a space to find comfort, hope and ideas to carry with you every day. This is a book of you, a place to spill all your secrets and fears, something to give you a jump in the morning and push you to explore your dreams, figure out who you are, or who you want to be. To help you to embrace the extremes of every emotion or hide inside its pages when you feel like a coward.

These pages will be a constant reminder that you are unique and powerful and there is nobody else quite like you. I don't pretend to have all the answers, in the grand scheme of things I truly know fuck all, but I do have a load of questions that might help you find some of your own along the way. I'm going to answer them with you. We are in this together.

This isn't a book to sit nicely on a shelf in silence, like my mum or my English teacher would have wanted. This is a book that lives in your bag, your pocket and your heart. One to break the spine on (fuck it, do that right now, literally break the spine of the book), to open at a random page and rip, paint, burn or send a piece of you out into the world without fear.

This book will push you to go deep and be true to yourself. It will end up in fucking tatters if you do it right. I want to see what you make of it and then I want you to pass it on.
So, turn this book up to 11, listen loud or put some music on in the background, I'd hate for you to be reading it in silence.
(Playlist suggested on page 18.)

Dom

IDENTITY

EXPLORE WHO YOU ARE WITHOUT FEAR OR SHAME.

THIS BOOK BELONGS TO...

Take a minute to record who you are right now

and remember we all change.

You will change
throughout this book.

Name:
....

Age:
....

Pronouns:
....

Sexuality:
....

Thinking:
....

Feeling:
....

Fearing:
....

Loving:
....

Hating:
....

Wearing:
....

Listening:
....

Smelling:
....

Watching:
....

Wanting:
....

Now cut it out and stick it to the front.

Make this book yours.

LET'S GET TO KNOW EACH OTHER.
THIS SECTION IS DESIGNED SO THAT YOU CAN DIG DEEP
INTO THE THINGS THAT REALLY MAKE YOU, YOU.
I'M GOING TO ANSWER THE QUESTIONS WITH YOU.
WE'LL TAKE IT IN TURNS.
YOU GO, I GO; YOU GO, I GO. ET CETERA, ET CETERA...

TELL ME A HAPPY MEMORY

The birth of my baby sister. My nan came to look after
us when my mum went into the hospital.
I didn't sleep a wink. Every single
negative outcome raced through my
mind. But nevertheless, morning
came, dad took us to the hospital
and I saw her for the first time.
   She was shimmering, effervescent
      whilst wriggling around.
I remember thinking she looked like
      the Michelin man.
         She was beautiful.
      They told me her
         name was Isobel.

TELL ME A SAD MEMORY.

The first time I got punched in the face.
It felt like the whole world swallowed me up.
I hated it. I did nothing about it, I still feel
embarrassed. Masculinity seems to hurt a lot the
first time that you feel it in your jaw.

THE FIRST PERSON THAT TRULY UNDERSTOOD YOU.

Mr Vergette, my drama teacher.

THE FIRST SONG THAT LIT YOU UP.

Maggie May — Rod Stewart
My grandmother used to play it in the car when I was
little. She would tell me that he was my grandfather,
as my mum never knew her dad. I wholeheartedly
believed it, until one day (I was around 7) we were
in the supermarket at the checkout and out of the
corner of my eye I saw a Rod Stewart CD. I picked it
up and shouted, 'Nan, when is grandad coming home?'
Everyone burst out into laughter, my grandmother
was completely embarrassed and that was the day
when I found out that Rod Stewart was in fact NOT
my grandfather. Nevertheless he
sings great fucking songs.

A TIME YOU FELT HATED.

Twitter, 2021.

A TIME YOU FELT LOVED.

Adam, my best friend and guitar player,
    had my back in an argument once. I overheard him
defending me from another room. I felt so protected,
    like I belonged somewhere. I could have cried.

A TIME YOU FELT AT HOME AWAY FROM 'HOME'.

Thursday night. 11pm. 12th February 2020. The Hawley
Arms, Camden. Upstairs. Mum to my right, you lot to
my left. Pint of Stella in my hand. Soaking wet.
Screaming along to My Chemical Romance.

A WORD YOU WOULD USE TO DESCRIBE YOURSELF.

Energetic.

THE LAST TIME YOU DID SOMETHING
FOR THE FIRST TIME.

Wrote a book. Lol.

TO BE DIFFERENT IS TO BE THE BEST FUCKING THING HERE AND YOU WILL BE CELEBRATED FOR THAT. WRITE OR DRAW SOMETHING YOU LOVE ABOUT YOURSELF.→ NOW STICK IT TO YOUR WALL AND COME BACK TO IT WHEN YOU NEED IT.

Always
show
your
true
self
to
the
world.

List
five
things
that
represent
you.

1

2

3

4

5

WRITE THE SONGS THAT MAKE YOU HAPPY ALL OVER THIS PAGE. WRITE IN CIRCLES, NOT IN LINES. LISTEN TO THEM LOUD!

Sally Cinnamon
The Stone Roses

There She Goes
The La's

Linger
The Cranberries

Our Day Will Come
Amy Winehouse

Champagne Supernova
Oasis

Before I Forget
Slipknot

Blind
Korn

Machine Gun
Yungblud

Bodies
Sex Pistols

London Calling
The Clash

DO THE SAME HERE WITH THE SONGS THAT MAKE YOU WANT TO RAGE.

DRAW FIVE THINGS THAT BRING YOU JOY

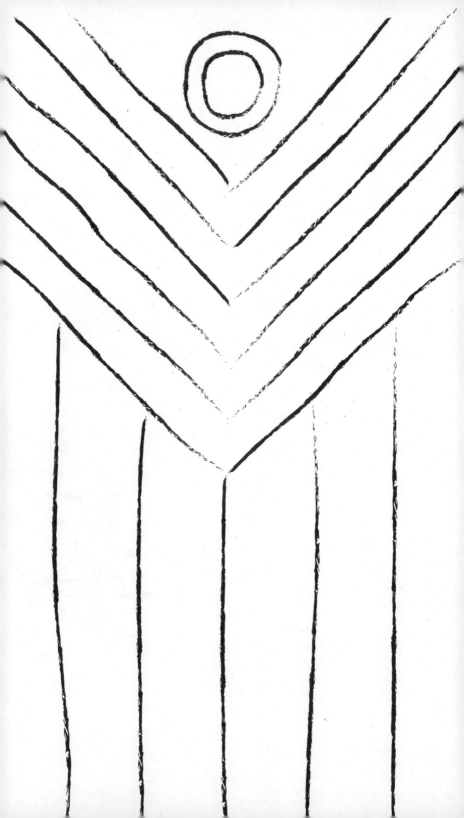

PAINT YOUR FLAG HERE WITH ANYTHING AND EVERYTHING. PAINT, PENS, BUTTONS, NAIL VARNISH, LIPSTICK, TAPE, WHATEVER YOU CAN GET YOUR HANDS ON.

WRITE DOWN 6 THINGS YOU LOVE ABOUT YOUR LIFE IN THE SQUARES BELOW.

CUT IT OUT, MAKE A DICE, ROLL IT EVERY DAY.

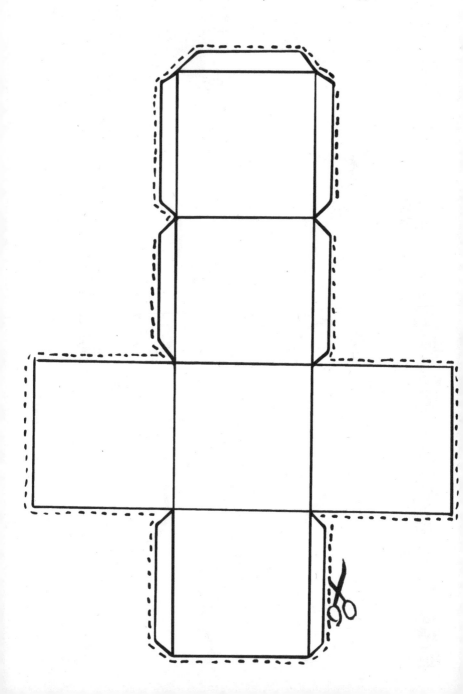

Don't show anyone for 30 days or they won't come true. Opinion kills instinct. (turn to page 92)

Take a break. Connect the creatures. Follow the route, make your own. Remember to enjoy the journey.

WRITE A MESSAGE TO YOUR YOUNGER SELF.

The shit you're going through right now
will help you find your people and you will
CHANGE THE WORLD TOGETHER.

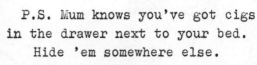

P.S. Mum knows you've got cigs
in the drawer next to your bed.
Hide 'em somewhere else.
DICKHEAD!

Write a message to yourself RIGHT NOW.
What do you need to hear?

Stop listening to everyone's opinion.
You're wasting time.
You know what you fucking want.
Your direction shouldn't be dependent on how
other people feel.

Make the fucking album you've been
wanting to make for two years.
Make **IDOLS**.
Fuck everyone else.
Stop diverting.
They are wrong.

WRITE A MESSAGE TO YOUR FUTURE SELF. SOMETHING YOU ALWAYS WANT TO KEEP HOLD OF.

I hope you truly lead with your heart and are happy with the outcome because it could never have been any other way.

WRITE NEGATIVE THOUGHTS HERE.
THEN RIP THE PAGE OUT AND BURN THEM.

 LET THEM FUCKIN GO.

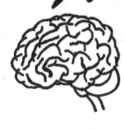

NOW DO THE SAME
WITH POSITIVE THOUGHTS.

DRAW, PAINT AND STICK THINGS IN. MAKE IT BIGGER AND BRIGHTER THAN THE LAST PAGE.

DON'T BURN
THIS ONE.

Creativity doesn't come
from a clean piece
of paper and
a new pen.

it's all around you,

floating above
your head.
There is Beauty
in the
Dirt.

Make
whatever
you
want
out of
whatever
you
want.

WRITE A POEM ABOUT SOMETHING THAT HAPPENED TO YOU TODAY RIGHT HERE. MAKE IT GRITTY, THINK JOHN COOPER CLARKE.

I saw a leaf, it gave me grief...

The Camel Blues

You gave me your number
 on a pack of camel blues
but I won't be able to pursue it
because I'm in love oh so in love

 I miss the adventure
That rabbit run in shoes
but i am in love oh so in love

You work in insurance
So I'm sure you'll appreciate the skew
 My heart's in a car crash but
it will never be for you

You gave me your number
 on a pack of camel blues
I got the camel blues for you
But I'm in love oh so in love …

EMPTY YOUR POCKETS ON THIS PAGE.

NOW DRAW AROUND EVERYTHING YOU FIND.

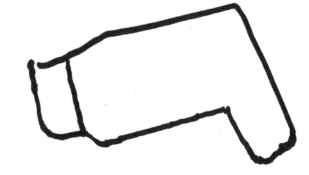

Fill this page
with things you want to learn.
Now, I challenge you to achieve
AT LEAST ONE of them this year.

Fill this page with things you want to see.

Now, again, I challenge you to see at least **ONE** of them this year.

READ BACK THROUGH YOUR ANSWERS SO FAR AND TAKE A MINUTE TO EMBRACE WHO YOU ARE.

YOU ARE UNIQUE.

NOW ROLL THIS
BOOK UP
INTO A TUBE
AND SCREAM
THROUGH IT
AS LOUD AS
YOU CAN.

I AM HERE.

CELEBRATE WHAT MAKES YOU DIFFERENT

SPEAK THE truth aND create iN THE WaY ONLY YOU CAN

Nothing stifles your power more than the fear of ~~making a mistake.~~

We are all battling against that voice that tells us we aren't good enough. The fear of other people's opinions, the fear of getting it 'wrong'.

So much energy and so many amazing ideas are lost through that fear.

I want this section to help you fucking

eradicate that fear.

Speak up in the way that only you can. Celebrate your

unique point of view at every opportunity.

Share it with the world.

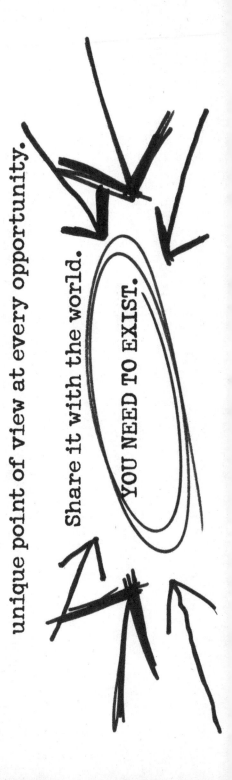

YOU NEED TO EXIST.

I battle fear by embracing it,
   I allow myself to know it's there.
   I listen to it and talk back,
as if it was a person in the room with me.
That's the fun in any good argument,
   you will learn something from both sides.
Even if the thing you are arguing with is
   the other side of your own head.
   When I'm scared about doing something,
sometimes I literally write the scenario
out as if it was a movie scene.
           It helps me rationalise what
                I'm going through.
                   Give it a try.

Think of something you are fearful
           of and start talking.
   Ask yourself why and really listen.
Write it down like a movie script.
      Two separate characters.
      You and your fear.
   Be detailed as fuck, don't let me down,
           it's time to win an Oscar
   - what happens at the end?
           You tell me.

Situation:

Setting:

Time of day:

Enter "fear" stage right.

Enter "you" stage left.

You:

Your Fear:

You:

Your Fear:

You:

Your Fear:

Decision:

DRAW A SMILEY FACE HERE
NEXT TO MINE.

THIS IS THE ONLY ONE LIKE THIS
IN THE WHOLE WORLD.

REMEMBER THAT YOU ARE SPECIAL.

Set a timer for one minute and write every
word that comes into your head.
Don't try and make it make sense,
just let your mind pour out onto this page.
I'll go first:

Camel thatched roofs

don't allow you to

talk to snowmen

because everyone will get hurt

when if the fire touches them

it's a slippery slope

more slippy than Fairy liquid

you could break your leg

and that would be bad…

WHAT THE FUCK IS IN MY HEAD???

Now your turn. Timer set? 3,2,1... GO!

STILL THINK YOU CAN'T WRITE?
MAKE A STORY USING THESE WORDS:

CLOWN

VEGAN

COFFIN

MOTOR CAR

STRAWBERRY LACE

PEAR TREE

TAKE A BREAK.
CURL THE BOOK INTO A HEART SHAPE
AND LOOK THROUGH IT.
TELL ME WHAT YOU CAN SEE.

DO IT AGAIN,
DIP THE END OF
THE BOOK IN INK
OR PAINT
AND STAMP
THE HEART
SHAPE
ON A
WALL.
YOU
CAN
MAKE
ART
OUT OF
ANYTHING.

WRITE A FUCKED UP THOUGHT HERE. SOMETHING THAT WOULD GET YOU "CANCELLED." REMEMBER THERE'S NO COMMENT SECTION IN THIS BOOK. IT'S JUST YOU AND ME.

Woah, you're fucked up lol. Now rip it out,
burn it and let's never talk of this again.

FILL
THIS
PAGE
WITH
GHOSTS.

GET A NEEDLE AND THREAD AND SEW UP ALL THE LIPS ON THIS PAGE.

EVERY TIME YOU FIND THE COURAGE TO SPEAK UP, COME BACK HERE AND CUT A THREAD.

What are you scared of people knowing about you?
Write it here. Now scream it out the window.

FUCK THAT FEAR.

I feel like I'm fat.

I don't like the bottom of my stomach.

It's always in the back of my mind

and I have to hide it.

I hate it.

Cover these pages in things that are your favourite colour.

TaKe a BReaK

FiLL tHis Page

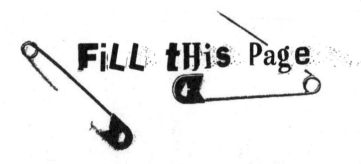

witH safety PiNs.

pieRce tHeM

tHROugH tHe PaPer.

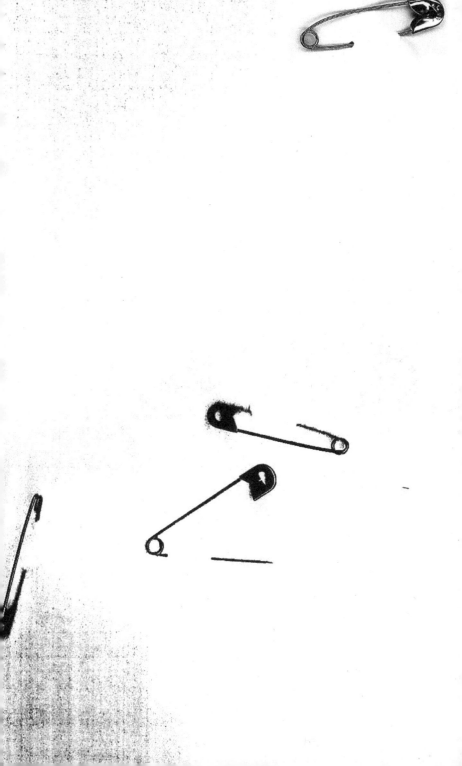

Lay this book open on a table. Play the drum set.

Clothes can make us feel powerful. They allow us to communicate who we are without saying any words at all. Draw the clothes that make you feel powerful, sexy and truly YOU. Find images on the internet, in magazines, ANYWHERE! Then collage the fuck out of this page.

Make it a moodboard. Start your own line right here.

I challenge you to wear something that you've found here every day for a week.

Go stand in front of the mirror and repeat after me.

NOBODY HAS EVER TOUCHED THE SKY WITHOUT JUMPING.

STOP CONFUSING INFORMATION WITH KNOWLEDGE.

TRUST YOUR GUT. FOLLOW YOUR NOSE. IT'S NOT THAT DEEP.

THE MORE YOU THINK, THE LESS YOU DO. THE LESS YOU DO,
THE MORE YOU THINK.

IF YOU'RE ONLY 60 PERCENT YOURSELF, YOU'RE ONLY GONNA FIND
PEOPLE WHO ARE 60 PERCENT RIGHT FOR YOU.

THERE'S NOTHING WRONG WITH BEING A CUNT
AS LONG AS YOU MEAN IT.

THE REASON YOU FEEL THIS WAY RIGHT NOW IS... TEMPORARY.

YOU ARE NOT YOUR THOUGHTS.

DON'T LET YOUR FEAR STAND INSIDE YOU, LET IT STAND BESIDE YOU.

IF YOU'RE DEPRESSED, BE DEPRESSED.
IF YOU'RE EXCITED, BE EXCITED.
WEAR YOUR EMOTIONS ON YOUR SLEEVE.

STEAL YOUR OWN SUNSHINE. ONCE YOU'VE GOT IT, SHARE IT WITH
YOUR MATES.

THE ONLY PERSON STANDING IN YOUR WAY IS YOU, SO GET OUT THE
WAY, YOU FUCKING IDIOT!

STOP TALKING SHITE, GO PLANT A TREE.

Write your own lyrics here.

BREAKDOWN!

DON'T FORGET
TO PUT YOUR FEET IN THE GRASS...
TELL YOUR MUM THAT YOU LOVE HER
SAY YOU CLEANED UP YOUR ACT!
GIVE MONEY TO THE HOMELESS MAN
HELP HIM BUY A BAR
WHEN YOU BUY YOUR MORNIN COFFEE
ASK 'EM HOW THEY ARE...

GOD SAVE THE SUNDAY MORNING
PRAY 4 ME ON THE SATURDAY NIGHT
TALK POLITE!
DON'T START FIGHTS!
DON'T TELL LIES!
THATS FOR THE PEOPLE WITH OBLIVIOUS
SHORT SIGHT.
ONE DAY WE'LL MEET AND I'LL SAY ALRGT!

SEE,
THE WORLD IS PRETTY BIG MAN
BUT DONT FEEL SMALL IN IT!
SOMETIMES YOU LOOSE A NUMBER BUT,
I SWEAR YOU'RE STILL CALLIN IT
I PROMISE YOU IT'll BE ALRIGHT IN THE END

FUCK THE DEPRESION!!!

ITS ALL IN YOUR HEAD, STAY WITH YOUR FRIENDS
AND WALK UP THE HILL AT QUARTER TO SIX
IN THE MORNING
TAKE IN THE AIR WHILST EVERYONE
IS STILL SNORING
EXPRESS YOURSELF WITH YOUR FRIENDS
(THEY'LL SAVE YOUR LIFE YOU KNOW?)
EVERYTHINGS ABOUT CONNECTION

YOU DONT HAVE TO BE ALONE!!!

LiFe iS a FiGHt

EMBRACING EMOTIONS IN ALL THEIR EXTREMES

I, **Dominic Richard Harrison,** am riddled head to toe with ADHD.

I love it and I fucking hate it. With ADHD the highs in my life are really high and the lows are extremely low.

I spend every day on a rollercoaster.

It can be really exhausting because I get overwhelmed by anxiety, pain and sadness really easily. It's like they're a big bald henchman waiting by the door of the restaurant I'm in, letting me know that in ten minutes he's going to drive me down to the river - use your imagination, you know what happens next.

It can be really hard for people close to me to understand because my emotional state moves so quickly, they often get left behind. They will still be processing some dark shit I said 10 minutes ago and then I'll walk into the room spritely like a bunny rabbit, wondering why they're not on my wavelength too. It then makes it hard for people to believe that what I am feeling in that moment is even real at all. I call them my sub emotions, stepping stone emotions that I go through to arrive at how I really feel. I know, fucking mental, right?

This is something that I live with. It's never going to change so I have to get to grips with it and work on it. I've found that if I am ever overwhelmed and scatter brained all I need to do is ground myself. It's impossible to think clearly if you feel like there is no reality around you. I walk out to the garden or a park and put my feet in some grass.

If I go buy a coffee, I make a conscious effort to smell it and taste it.
If I'm on the street, I go and touch a wall. I use my senses and they ground me.
Yes, I look weird as fuck doing it! But so what? It helps me.

We all get so wrapped up in a million different things we forget the simple
beauty all around us, like how amazing our senses are. To be able to breathe,
touch, smell, hear and taste is a gift. Breathe in right now, go on,
proper deep – do it. Do it again.

How sick does that feel? How lucky are we that we get to do that
all day every day?

We forget and we take it for granted.
I think when I apply that way of thinking to my life, it provides something
I can control inside a world of shit I cannot
– it makes the hard times easier.

Try it ...

Now, get outside and let me know what you:

Smelt:

Tasted:

Heard:

Touched:

Today these simple actions took you out of your head for a second and brought you back down to earth.

Take it a step further, make this page smell of something.
Spray perfume. Drip a candle on it.
Crush up an incense stick and rub it in.
Washing detergent, anything that
will ground you.
Come back here when you need it.

Happiness

I have always felt
that if I'm happy
I'll get complacent.
Happiness is scary
because you feel
like it's all about
to go wrong. It's OK
to find happiness,
it's OK to feel it.

I hope you find a
little bit of it in this.
When you start to
fear happiness,
turn to this page
and remember:

YOU

deserve it.
Everyone does.

OPINION KILLS INSTINCT.

I believe that instinct is the most powerful form
of expression. It's your subconscious giving you an
answer before any rationalisation, anxiety or logical
thought comes into play. It's your body leading in
its rawest most animalistic form. Trust it or at least
listen to it. Allow it to be a part of the argument
when it comes to your decision making. Opinions can
be very dangerous. If you pay too much attention
to them, they can lead you to a place where you start
to shut down your instinct automatically.
You start to believe that there is something wrong
with it or you trick yourself into thinking another
person's thought or idea is your own.
    You have to create a boundary in your mind.
Listen to the opinions, know that they are there,
but take a step back, put them next to your own
instinct and thoughts, THEN decide.
Only you will know what is best for you at the
end of that process.

NOW WRITE A LIST OF THE OPINIONS THAT YOU'VE PROVED WRONG.

Come back here when you doubt yourself.
Or when you're weighing an opinion too heavily.

SOMEBODY ONCE ASKED ME WHY I DON'T LET THE NEXT TIME YOU FIND AN OPINION WEIGHING ON YOU. TRY IT OUT THE NEXT TIME REMEMBER THAT AND TRY IT OUT NEVER HAVE POWER OVER ME. REMEMBER THAT LONG AS I KNOW THE ANSWER. THEY CAN NEVER HAVE POWER OVER ME.

OPINIONS OF OTHERS SHAKE ME. THE TRUTH IS I ACTUALLY DO LET THEM SHAKE ME. OPINIONS MAKE ME LOOK IN THE MIRROR AND ASK MYSELF IF THEY ARE TRUE OR NOT. AS LONG AS YOU KNOW THE TRUTH FUCK EVERYONE ELSE. NOW, JUMP ALL OVER THIS PAGE. REMEMBER YOU ARE POWERFUL

FUTURE

rippin'

(worrying about something that hasn't happened yet)

It's so easy to build up scenarios in your head based on what you believe other people's intentions

or feelings are. It's a dark thing our brains do that can lead us to self-sabotage without having any facts.

The best thing you can do is communicate,
     to others, and to yourself.
     When this happens to me,
     I write the scenario in my head down on paper. Most of the time, when I read them in black and white, they seem fucking ridiculous, and it brings me back down to reality. When you find yourself future trippin', write down what you're worried about below.

SLEEP WITH ME NEXT TO YOU OR UNDER YOUR PILLOW. OPEN TO THIS PAGE WHEN YOU WAKE UP EVERY MORNING FOR A WEEK AND FOLLOW THESE INSTRUCTIONS:

DAY 1: Tell me how you feel.

Now get the fuck out of bed and tell someone you love them

DAY 2: Tell me how you feel.

Now stand in front of the mirror and repeat after me.

What am I going through right now?

Will it matter in a year?

Will it matter in a month?

Will it matter in a week?

DAY 3: Tell me how you feel.

Now go for a run.
Do some exercise, get your blood pumping!

Buy an alien or Halloween mask,
no matter what time of year it is. Stand in it for a while.
Look out your window and fuck with some people.

DAY 4: Tell me how you feel.

Now go outside and look up at the sky. Find a cloud.
Think about how many people are looking at the same sky
right now. Do you think the clouds look the same from
their point of view? Remember you aren't alone.

DAY 5: Tell me how you feel.

Now go and buy yourself flowers, a scented candle,
or some incense - the vibes will go up drastically,
I promise.

DAY 6: Tell me how you feel.

Stand barefoot in the grass today. Ground yourself.

DAY 7: Tell me how you feel.

Stay in bed today. Take a day off.
No one likes a try hard!

Write down a time you felt let down

NOW BURN THIS PAGE
AND LET THE PAIN GO.

WHAT ARE YOU AFRAID OF?

Write yours here.

Spikey chairs

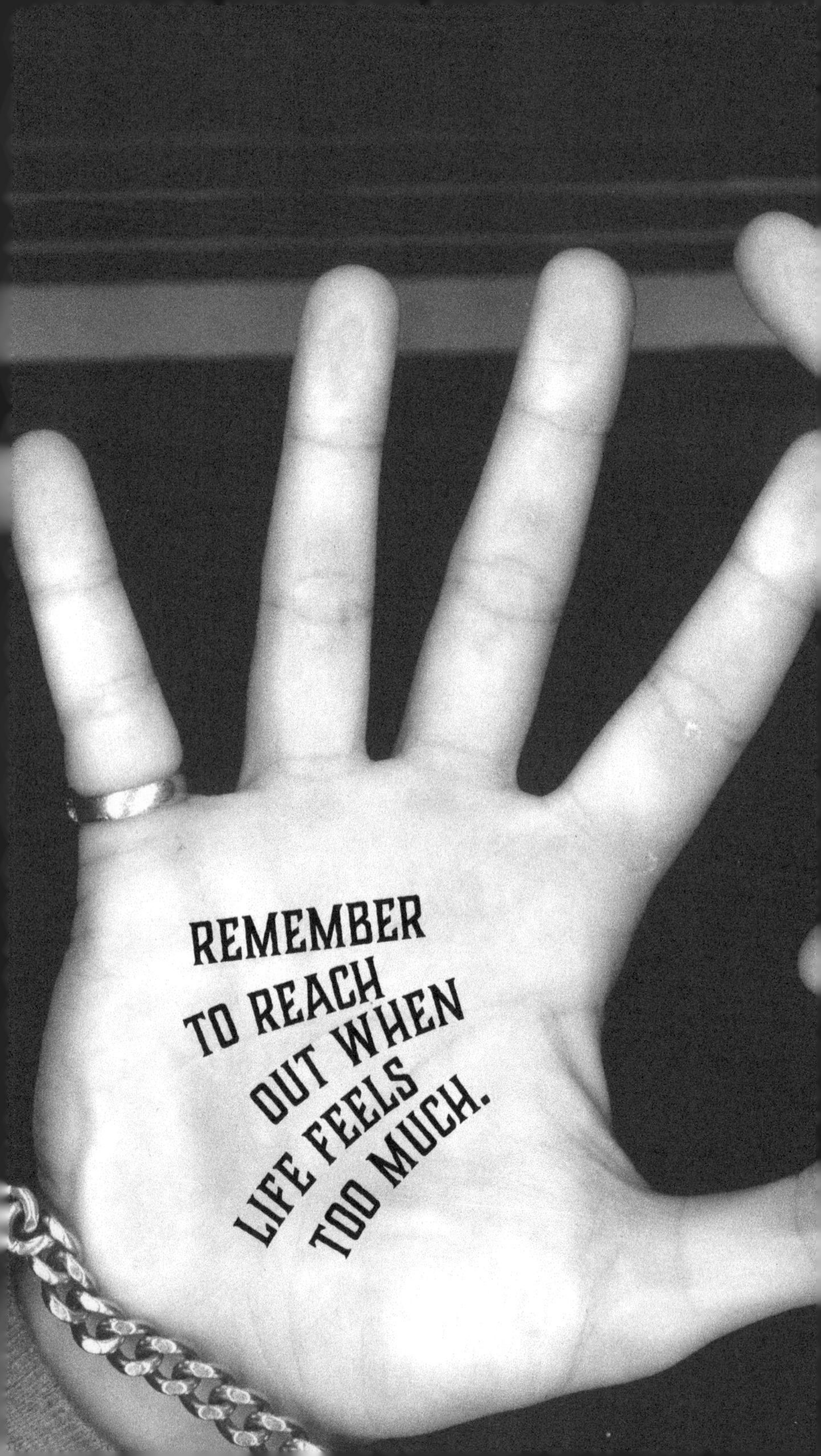
REMEMBER
TO REACH
OUT WHEN
LIFE FEELS
TOO MUCH.

PUT YOUR
HANDS ON MINE,
SIT WITH ME
AND BREATHE
THROUGH IT.

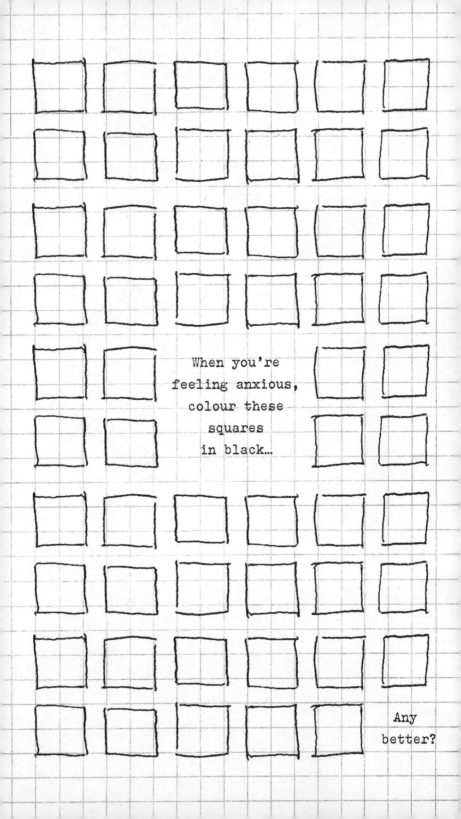

When you're
feeling anxious,
colour these
squares
in black...

Any
better?

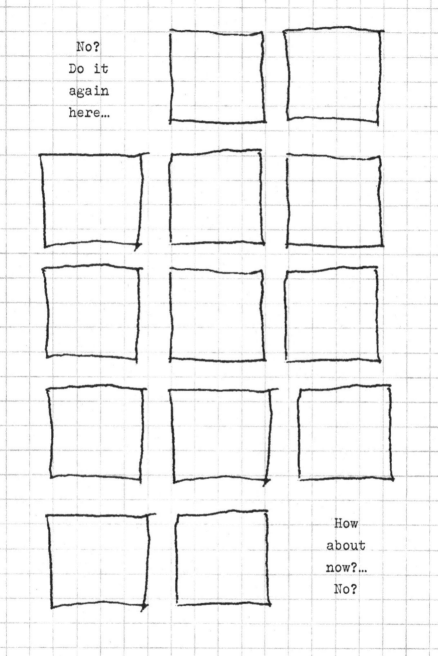

No?
Do it
again
here...

How
about
now?...
No?

Fuck the squares, now do the whole page.
And the next one.
Keep going if you need to.

I find it really hard to sleep. The idea of not sleeping keeps me awake.

I often find myself staring at the ceiling, counting the hours until I've got to be up.

"Five hours till I have to wake up, four hours, three hours, etc, etc..."

However, I think I've found a solution...

Can't sleep? Count the sheep.

Smoking sheep

Naked sheep

Devil sheep

Plain sheep

Still awake? Chances are so am I. It's alright, go make a cuppa tea, camomile for me ...

Punk sheep

Sheemo

Black sheep

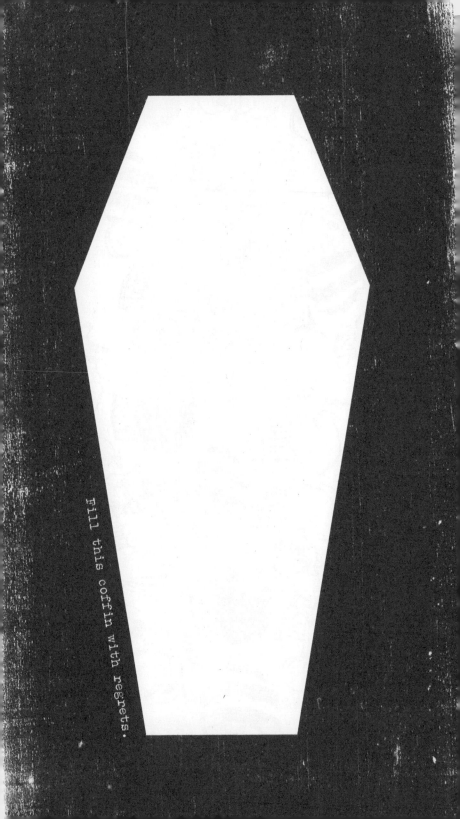

Fill this coffin with regrets.

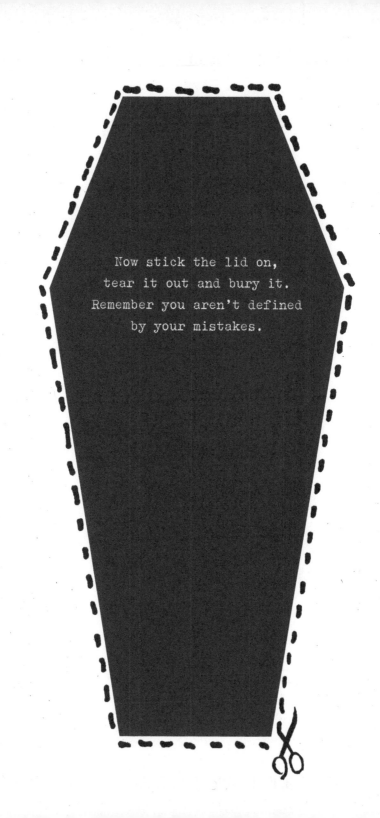

Now stick the lid on,
tear it out and bury it.
Remember you aren't defined
by your mistakes.

WRITE FIVE THINGS YOU HATE ABOUT THE WORLD HERE.

NOW SLAM THE BOOK SHUT AND THROW IT ACROSS THE ROOM.

NOW PICK IT UP AND WRITE TEN THINGS
YOU LOVE ABOUT THE WORLD TOO.

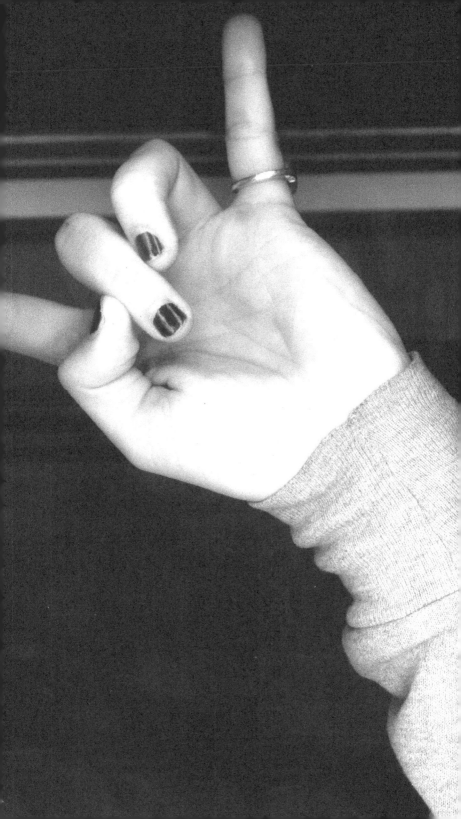

When you're angry,
scribble here
until you break
through the page!

WHEN
THIS BOOK
is fUCKeD
aND faLLiNg
aPaRt,
gET sOMe taPe
aND PUt iT
BacK
tOgetHeR.

Remember
broken
things
are
beautiful.

A PAGE ON HEARTBREAK

Heartbreak sucks.

I hate it.

But it is necessary.
You will never have a bigger growth spurt
than when you get your heart broken.

You have to remember who you are without another person.

If you're going through it right now, I'm sorry.

If you have never felt it, you will and I'm sorry in advance.

But on the bright side, it is amazing fuel for poetry.

I never really share this side of my writing but at the end of the day
I am trying my best to write a book – so fuck it!

I hope this helps:

missin somebody is a very strange thing

it's like there's a step at the top of the stair

but the step is elsewhere, I'm treading thin air

for a second I can feel your breath and your hair

but then I put my foot down and there's just nothing there

everyone around says be careful so rationally

but if I try to rationalise the way I feel then it just turns into anxiety

I feel sorry for them because they'll never understand

yeah, they're tryna protect my heart

but I felt I was protected just by touching your hand

for as long as I can remember I was lost in my own head

like a penny down a drain no one would try to collect

who knew you would come along and so gracefully intercept

my fragile heart with your cigarette break intellect

I think about playin dot to dot with the freckles on your face,

as I pull down your underwear and join up two symmetrical birthmarks

just below your waist while I'm sat here, I know you're sat there

I'm trying to make eye contact across millions of miles of thin air

As blind as a bat, I still feel your stare as it shoots down my back

– it helps me repair in my imagination.

Suddenly we clock eyes, you throw me a wink and I know it will

all be alright I know it's not real and I'm out of your sight,

But it hurts oh so much

So I'll just imagine tonight.

Tell
your
family
something
you
wish
they
knew.

It wasn't an easy upbringing,
it hurt, but it fucking happened, and it's made me who I am.
I could go into details for the sake of everyone's
entertainment, but I feel like I've already done that
and what I really want to say now is: to every one of you,
I'm sorry for all the bullshit we've been through.
I forgive you, I love you and I hope you can forgive me too.

If you're worried about a relationship,
coming out, falling for someone,
breaking up with someone or anything
to do with that big fuck off word that is

LOVE

then remember this:

It's scary for all of us.
If someone tells you they're not scared
they are lying.

You cannot live your life based on the
expectations of others. Their expectations
of you are never going to be your own.

EVER.

Underline it.
Tattoo it to the inside of your eyelids.

You will change, everything will twist and turn
because you will learn more.

Put yourself in an environment where you are open to change, even if nothing happens to your fundamentals. That's how you will truly be able to figure it out.

Fuck it. Try things, you never know.

It's complicated. You will feel a million things all at once but give it time and your true feelings will rise to the surface. Listen to your gut, it's way wiser than your brain.

LOVE is shit, dirty, riddled with anxiety, a looooooooooooooooooooooooong journey but it's the most beautiful thing in the world so be present and enjoy the ride.

To obtain LOVE you have to do one thing, that's be yourself. If you are not yourself you will never truly find it.

GOOD LUCK.

Write the names of people you love

(or want to love) here.

Now go and tell them.

FIND YOUR COMMUNITY

FIGHTING LONELINESS AND LEADING WITH LOVE

Wow, I never knew we would get on so well.
Thank you for opening up to me.
This is how this whole thing (Yungblud) started.
I felt like for 17 years of my life I was shouting
into a black void

"IS THERE ANYONE ELSE
OUT THERE WHO FEELS
THE SAME WAY AS ME?"

I never thought that if I made that void on my iPhone,
millions of you would respond.
We've kind of just been winging it, telling each other
the truth without hesitation for eight years now
and 10 people turned into 10 million.
That's how I found my community.
What the fuck!?

The biggest lesson I've learned from all this is
that if you feel strongly about something, you have
to communicate it because there is definitely someone
out there who feels exactly the same way as you
but if you say nothing, you will never find each
other, because you will never know.

The thing you need to understand is that Yungblud
is not just me. It's me, it's you, it's us.
It's something we all have in common.
A movement that allows people to find each other
by being 100% themselves, because if you're
only 50% yourself then you will only find people
who are 50% right for you. You have to
put your true self out there.

Community is constant.

Trends will change.

People will come and go.

YOU might come and go.

But a community like this
will always be here for you
when you decide to come back.

LOVE
IN
THE
FACE
OF
HATE.

Throughout my childhood and especially now,
I receive a lot of hate and misunderstanding
for the way I express myself,the way I dress
and the way I communicate.
Hate, first hand.
Something I walk side by side with every day.
It makes you feel as if you're not real.
A character. Stripped of all dignity,
desperate for connection and any sort of validation.
You just want to feel loved.
Truly loved.
I learned that I can't control how other people
respond to me. The only thing that I can actually
control is the way I treat others.
It starts with me.
I feel love by loving them.
I don't mean in some Cupid fucking fairytale kind of way,
I mean by radiating it as much as I can,
by being present and giving a shit.

Once you start this process, you soon realise that
the validation you so desperately seek
is within yourself. The more you love others,
the more you will love life,
and the more they/you will love you.

INSECURITY IS A FENCE. JUMP OVER IT.

Love as hard as you can every day,
give a little bit to everyone you meet,
it's like a muscle,
the more you use it, the stronger it will get.
That is how we beat
"the loneliness"
and
"the darkness."
Love even if they don't reciprocate,
it doesn't matter,
you're further ahead in the journey than they are.
Love is power.
Love is everything we all want,
in all its forms.
Look at me,
the fucking hippy.

The next time someone is shit to you,
give them love back and then watch the confusion
on their face - it's hilarious.

FILL THIS PAGE WITH KISSES.
HERE'S ONE FROM ME TO YOU.

TAKE THIS WITH YOU TO A GIG. FIND SOME MATES IN THE LINE OUTSIDE AND GET THEM TO WRITE THEIR NAMES HERE.

KEEP GOING UNTIL IT'S FULL OF THE NAMES OF PEOPLE
BROUGHT TOGETHER BY MUSIC.

Write the names of your chosen family here.

Now draw something that reminds you of each of them.

**PLAY A GAME OF CONSEQUENCES HERE.
I'LL START WITH A LINE, THEN FOLD THE PAGE UP TO COVER
THE LINE AND WRITE YOUR OWN, THEN PASS IT ROUND WITH
MATES AND KEEP GOING UNTIL THE PAGE IS FULL.**

I've just seen my ex best friend across the room.
We haven't spoken for six months and we're at the
same party. They haven't seen me yet.

Swap this book with someone for a week. Come back together and see what each of you has made of it. We've all got our unique spin on things.

FILL THIS PAGE♥ WITH HEARTS. NOW TEAR THEM OUT & GIVE 'EM ♥ ♥♥ OUT TO STRANGERS. ♥ ♥ ♥ ♥ ♥

TAKE SOMETHING FROM A PLACE YOU FEEL AT HOME AND STICK IT HERE. CARRY A PIECE OF IT WITH YOU.

I'M TALKING GIGS OR TRAIN TICKETS, BEER MATS, A DOODLE, A LEAF, A NAPKIN, A POSTCARD... ANYTHING.

INTRODUCE
yOURSELF TO someOne
NEW TODAY.

SMILE AT PEOPLE YOU

MAKE EYE CONTACT WITH.

How did it go?
How did you feel?
Tell me here.

Write a message of love for a stranger here.
Now tear it out and leave it somewhere
it will be found.

PLAY A GAME OF "THIS" OR "THAT" WITH YOURSELF.

LEFT OR RIGHT

NIGHT OR DAY

UP OR DOWN

BLACK OR WHITE

ODD OR EVEN

LIGHT OR DARK

PENCIL OR PAINT

FILM OR TV

WALK OR RUN

SINK OR SWIM

TRUTH OR LIES

SUMMER OR WINTER

NOW PLAY IT WITH A STRANGER.

LEFT OR RIGHT

NIGHT OR DAY

UP OR DOWN

BLACK OR WHITE

ODD OR EVEN

LIGHT OR DARK

PENCIL OR PAINT

FILM OR TV

WALK OR RUN

SINK OR SWIM

TRUTH OR LIES

SUMMER OR WINTER

Write a poem about
somewhere you feel at home.

Stick pictures of the people
and places you love
here.

Now
graffiti all over them.
Names, dates, feelings, thoughts ...

Here's mine...

CAMDEN TOWN

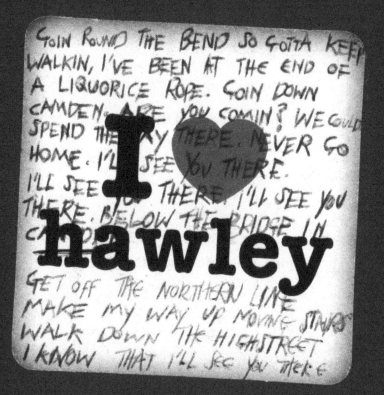

DON'T WANNA SPEND MY MONEY
ON FANCY CARS. I WANNA SIT RIGHT
HERE IN THE HAWLEY ARMS.
I WANNA DRINK MY BEER TO
FIX MY HEART COZ THEY DON'T
GIVE A SH WHO YOU ARE. BRING
YOUR DOG WITH THE BROKEN ARM.

I ♥ hawley

ONLY KOLLIES, NO CIGARS
ELLE'S GETTIN' ROWDY BEHIND THE
BAR. "YOU LOOK LIKE A LUVER WITH
        THAT GUITAR"

ITS SPECIAL SO SPECIAL
SO PECIAL. ALL THE PUNX N THE
FREAKS N THE DYKES N THE
TWINX YEH I FEEL IT DEEP
IN MY HEART. RAIN RAIN, DON'T
HAVE TO AWAY. LISTEN TO
WHAT I SAY. WATCH ME LIKE

I ♥ hawley

A LITTLE FLOWER...
I'LL SEE YOU THERE. I'LL SEE YOU
THERE. I'LL SEE YOU THERE
BELOW THE BRIDGE IN CAMDEN

PASS IT ON

YOU MADE IT. LET'S SEE WHO YOU ARE NOW.

FiLL
t#is Out
again &
stick it
tO tHe
frOnt
Of t#e
BOOK

Name: _____

Age: _____

Pronouns: _____

Sexuality: _____

Thinking: _____

Feeling: _____

Fearing: _____

Loving: _____

Hating: _____

Wearing: _____

Listening: _____

Smelling: _____

Watching: _____

Wanting: _____

BURY
THIS
BOOK.
DIG IT UP
ONE YEAR
FROM NOW,
SEE WHAT'S
WHAT'S
CHANGED.

THANKS FOR EXISTING.

Happy Place Books, an imprint of Ebury Publishing
20 Vauxhall Bridge Road London SW1V 2SA

Happy Place Books is part of the Penguin Random House group of companies
whose addresses can be found at global.penguinrandomhouse.com

Penguin
Random House
UK

First published by Happy Place Books in 2024

www.penguin.co.uk

A CIP catalogue record for this book
is available from the British Library

ISBN 9781529932065

Editor: Sam Crisp Design: Dave Brown - apeinc.co.uk

Printed and bound in Great Britain by Clays Ltd, Elcograf S.p.A.

The authorised representative in the EEA is Penguin Random House Ireland,
Morrison Chambers, 32 Nassau Street, Dublin D02 YH68

Penguin Random House is committed to a sustainable future for our business,
our readers and our planet. This book is made from Forest Stewardship
Council® certified paper.

If you find yourself struggling with any of the issues raised in this book then
please do reach out for support. Either to a health professional, friend or
family member but there are also helpful resources that can be found online.

MIX
Paper | Supporting
responsible forestry
FSC® C018179